Liminality

Devynn Major

Presentation by *BookLeaf Publishing*

Web: www.bookleafpub.com

E-mail: info@bookleafpub.com

ISBN: 9789357212854

First edition 2023

to my life's loves and losses. thank you.

6am / 11pm

The brief morning moments
of the first few days,
that's where I wanted to live.
Just before memory whispered
to wake up.

I drifted over afternoons
picking at the scabs on my heart
just for one look at your face.
I made my fingers bleed
digging for some piece of you
even after you'd gone.

I still impatiently wait for night
because at night I dream
and dreams aren't real.

oct 6

You call and I come.
Heart tight as my hands
on my steering wheel.
I can't fix you
and I'm so sorry.

I knew I would never see you like this again,
holding my face,
the gold wing around your neck
kissing my lips,
because it felt like goodbye.

I'll write you a love letter
you'll never read,
and in it I'll say thank you
for leaving me more beautiful
than when you found me.

don't be sweet

The ghost of your voice will
visit me sometimes,
Other nights I can't remember your laugh.
That's when I desperately search my apartment
for some token of you.
I find you in my cupboards
my unfolded clothes
the warmth of my shower,
except you're not smiling.

I'm slow
dragging every bit of you in
from wherever I unearth it.
It will be a while until I can't carry any more,
so I remain.

If it's not you stepping on my chest
then who is it?

liminality

I existed next to myself
for six short weeks
that stretched on forever.

Holding me there,
a kite on a string.
Not quite here
not quite not.
I thought,
"It's beautiful up here"
but I couldn't convince myself.

I asked you to let me go
or pull me back,
so I slipped away,
deflating in my descension,
and someday soon I'll think again,
"It's beautiful down here"
and I'll believe it.

within & without

Some days I don't know
where I am.
You held me still
like a paperweight,
so I wouldn't float away.
There's nothing holding me now
and some days I don't know
where I am.

inside

I've hidden myself
in rain streaking windows,
quiet glimpses of sun
only seen in reflection.
All at once here, and not.

Lowly, I've watched little tears
decorate your eyes -
hands wrung tight.
I'm the dust atop
your favourite book,
its pages dog-eared and worn.
In here, awaiting a second glance
when you recognize me
because I hadn't left.

what's mine is mine

Here she is
soft and sweet and
holding me.
She is a swollen eye,
a split lip
a dark bruise,
cold hands.

She takes me places
on foot,
in dreams,
through water,
never alone.
Not for a moment.

I won't have her forever
and somehow that's okay
when there is no other choice.

love letter

My home is a shrine to my own heart.
I live in a love letter
I've written to myself.

Thin curls of my hair
collecting on the carpet,
loose threads of my
favourite sweater.
The smell of burning coffee
mixed with lavender
mixed with stillness
and only me breathing it all.

at home, at home

What does it mean when
in my head I hear
"I want to go home"
But I'm sitting here, on my bed?

Where can I take you
if not here?

Home is not a person anymore
it's you

A Funeral, Twice

Cover me, Daddy
cover the losses
the woes, and the rot.

Pooling dark bleeds my
eyes, until a breath of dawn
relights them. The hour I've forgotten you.

But I clawed at your grained skin -
desperate to leave tiny splinters
in my fingers to remember you by.

The bees outside my mouth
have stopped making honey, Dad.
Why did you send them away?

ossuary

Bring me, in your hearse
to the graveyard
where words fell from you
with some miserable thud.
Where they combed through the grass
and you watched them hold me
and you let them hold me
and I won't ever open my mouth again.

Your house is underground.
I live there now.
I live in night terrors
wearing another's face.
You don't live here anymore.
I've taken your place
so you should thank me,
but you won't.

I am choking in the hands of your past self,
watching in the mirror.
You promised you'd never leave me.

a house is not a home

I've been caught on skinned knees
flushed red.
I've been in love
and love is a derelict house
roof caving in,
but brand new wallpaper
in one room.

a well

can you hear me
way down here
buried beneath myself?
pull me out
in sweet mornings,
wide awake at noon.
just promise
you'll put me back to sleep.

five of cups

I wake in shambles
my mouth is upside down
and my pulse is a mess.
I've been straining
to listen for water.

Today was ashes.
Today was a puddle at your feet.

you can hold my hand if you want to

IV
you touch me and you've left the keys in the
ignition
I'm on fire and you put me here.

I
how did you find me?
you follow the words you're afraid to use
I watch your eyes trace them like calligraphy,
like you're learning cursive.

II
I feel your eyes on my mouth, you're not hiding.
the soft heat of your body nearly kissing mine.
I lift your face up and your pupils dilate,
bass floods around me but I can hear your
breath.
what time is it?

III
you steal bitter air and return it warm. for me?
I won't ask you.
your body has curled for me, smaller, so you can
hear me,
touch me gently, an accident?
I won't ask you.

IV.II
lay upside down, don't let my hair fall
from your hands,
devour me at 3am
beside me and below me and above me.
I can take you, too.
tell me to and I'll eat you whole.

little bones

my god you're thin
I think as I hold your face for the first time
in months.
my palm fits in the hollow of your cheek.
you're a skeleton, but I can still feel
the same weight when you kiss me.
I can see your ribs and I want to cry.

you're bones.

I have you now but then you'll go
find god somewhere else
because he wasn't in my mouth
and you knew that.

-

you're always in my dreams now
and I want to yell at you to get out,
but not as bad as I want
to lay beside you in them.

X

I don't think you're poison
when you tear through
my stomach,
my swollen lips

I can taste it
and I'll bleed anyway

sunsetting

I saw some flowers
in the garden
they made me
think of you.
They were you,
all of them
were all of you.

iv

I wanted to write you a sonnet
but I didn't know how
to fit the words in my mouth.

Wrapping me in
a strange blanket of
the darkest parts of you,
I saw you cry the day
I met you.
Showed me and brought me
and kept me there,
and when it was done
you threw the blanket out
with me.

13

Bend to take me,
quiet the shaking of my limbs,
touch the pads of your fingers
to my eyelids

Lift a hollow body
and place it next to you,
tilt its head to the sun
for one small warmth

One kiss left from here
Sweetness, even in death